The Poetry of Bliss Carman

Volume X - Pipes of Pan No I. From the Book of Myths

William Bliss Carman was born in Fredericton, in New Brunswick on April 15th 1861. He was educated at Fredericton Collegiate School before moving to the University of New Brunswick, obtaining his B.A. there in 1881. As is common with so many writers his first published piece was for the University magazine and for Carman that was in 1879.

After several years editing various magazines and periodicals Carman first published a poetry volume in 1893 with Low Tide on Grand Pré. There was no Canadian company prepared to publish and when an American company did so it went bankrupt.

The following year was decidedly better. His partnership with the American poet Richard Hovey had given birth to Songs of Vagabondia. It was an immediate success.

That success prompted the Boston firm, Stone & Kimball, to reissue Low Tide on Grand Pré and to hire Carman as the editor of its literary journal, The Chapbook.

Carman brought out, in 1895, Behind the Arras, a somewhat more serious and philosophical work centered on the premise of a long meditation, using the speaker's house and its many rooms, as a symbol of life and the choices to be made.

In 1896 Carman met Mrs Mary Perry King, who rapidly became patron, adviser and sometime lover. She also became his writing collaborator on two verse dramas.

In 1897 Carman published Ballad of Lost Haven, and in 1898, By the Aurelian Wall, the title poem itself was an elegy to John Keats and the book was a collection of formal elegies.

As the century turned Carman was hard at work on a five-volume set of poetry "Pans Pipes". The excellence of a number of these poems did much to install Carman as the most noted of Canadian Poets and eventually their own Poet Laureate.

In 1912 the final work in the Vagabondia series was published. Richard Hovey had died in 1900 and so this last work was purely Carman's. It has a distinct elegiac tone as if remembering the past works themselves.

On October 28th, 1921 Carman was honored by the newly-formed Canadian Authors' Association where he was crowned Canada's Poet Laureate with a wreath of maple leaves.

William Bliss Carman died of a brain hemorrhage at the age of 68 in New Canaan on the 8th June, 1929.

Index of Contents

PREFACE

It is a hearty old saying that "Good wine needs no bush." Why, then, should the master of a road-house hang out a sign, letting folk know there is good drink within?

Consider the feelings of the landlord, poor man.
At once nettled and abashed, he exclaims:

"Pray why should I stick a bough over my door? My tavern is well bespoke for miles about, and all the folk know I serve nothing but good, honest liquor, and mighty comforting it is of a cold night, when the fire is bright on the hearth, or refreshing on a hot day either."

"Nay, but," says the stranger, "how should a traveller know of this? You must advertise, man. Hang out your sign to attract the passer-by, and increase trade. Trade's the thing. You should be doing a driving business, with a cellar like yours."

"Huh," replies the taverner, "I perceive that in the city where you come from it may not be a mark of character in a man to rely wholly upon merit, but that if one would ensure success, he must sound a trumpet before him, as the hypocrites do, that they may have glory of men, as the Word says."

"Tut, man," says the stranger, "look at your friend John Doe under the hill yonder. Does a wonderful business. Famous all over the country for his home-brewed ale, and his pockets lined with gold."

"Yes," says the host, "John Doe is a good thrifty man and as fine a comrade as you'd wish to find, selling his hundred thousand bottles a year. But the gist of the matter between us isn't all in quantity, I'll be bound. Quality is something. And as for myself I would as soon have a bottle of wine as a keg of beer any day. Wine is the poetry of life, in a manner of speaking, and ale you see is the prose, very good to get along on, but no sorcery in it. Three things, I always say, a man needs have, meat for his belly, a fire for his shins, and generous wine to keep him in countenance with himself. And that's no such easy matter in a difficult world, I can tell you. 'Tis wine that gives a man courage and romance, and puts heart in him for deeds and adventures and all manner of plain wholesome love. And that, after all, is the mainspring with most men, hide it how they may. For what ever was done, that was worth doing, and was not done for a woman or for the sake of a friend, I should like to know?"

"Maybe I hadn't thought of that," says the stranger. "You must have tasted some rare wine in your time."

"Not so much," says the other, "but I was born with a shrewd taste for it, you may say. Moreover I came of a people who were far farers in their day, and have been abroad myself more than once. So it comes you find the foreign vintages in my bins. There's some Greek wine I have, sir, that's more than a century old, I'll wager; and a rare Moon-wine, as they call it, picked up in an out-of-the-way port, that will make you forget your sorrow like a strain of music; light wines from France, too; and some Heather Brose, very old and magical, such as the little dark people used to make hereabout in the times of the Celts long ago, and very good times they were too. It is not these days that have all the wisdom ever was, you may be sure."

" You are not such a bad advocate, after all," remarks the stranger. " You speak very invitingly."

" Step inside," says the landlord.

Bliss Carman
The Ghost House,
Twilight Park in the Catskills,
August, 1902.

OVERLORD

Lord of the grass and hill,
Lord of the rain,
White Overlord of will,
Master of pain,

I who am dust and air
Blown through the halls of death,
Like a pale ghost of prayer,
I am thy breath.

Lord of the blade and leaf,
Lord of the bloom,
Sheer Overlord of grief,
Master of doom,

Lonely as wind or snow,
Through the vague world and dim,
Vagrant and glad I go;
I am thy whim.

Lord of the storm and lull,
Lord of the sea,
I am thy broken gull,
Blown far alee.

Lord of the harvest dew,
Lord of the dawn,
Star of the paling blue
Darkling and gone,

Lost on the mountain height
Where the first winds are stirred,
Out of the wells of night
I am thy word.

Lord of the haunted hush,
Where raptures throng,
I am thy hermit thrush,
Ending no song.

Lord of the frost and cold,
Lord of the North,
When the red Sun grows old
And day goes forth,

I shall put off this girth,
Go glad and free,
Earth to my mother earth,
Spirit to thee.

THE PIPES OF PAN

This is something that I heard,
Half a cry and half a word,
On a magic day in 'June,
In the ghostly azure noon,
Where the wind among the trees
Made mysterious melodies,
Such as those which filled the earth
When the elder gods had birth.

Ah, the world is growing old!
Of the joys it used to hold,
Love and beauty, naught have I
But the fragrant memory.

Once, ah, once, (ye know the story!)
When the earth was in her glory,
Ere man gave his heart to breed
Iron hate and heartless greed,
Near a meadow by a stream
Quiet as an ageless dream,
As I watched from the green rim
Of a beech grove cool and dim,
Musing in the pleasant shade
The soft leafy sunlight made,
What should gleam and move and quiver
Down by the clear, pebbly river,
Where the tallest reeds were growing
And the bluest iris blowing,
Gleam a moment and then pass,
(Ah, the dare-to-love she was,
In her summer-fervid dress
Of sheer love and loveliness!)
Wayward, melting, shy, and fond,
Lissome as a bulrush wand,
Fresh as meadowsweet new-blown,
Sandal lost, and loosened zone,
Our own white Arcadian
Touched with rose and creamy tan,
Eyes the colour that might fleck
The red meadow lily's neck,
Hair with the soft silky curl
Of some strayed patrician girl,
Beech-brown on the sunlit throat,
Cheek of tawny apricot,
Parted lips and breast aglow, —
Who but Syrinx, as ye know!

Gone, swift as a darting swallow,
What could young Pan do but follow?
(Have ye felt the warm blood leap,
When the soul awakes from sleep,
At a glance from some dark eye
Of a sudden passing by? —
Known the pulse's hurried throb
And the breathing's catch and sob,
When, upon his race with Death,
Life the runner halts for breath,
Taking with a happy cry
His brief draught of ecstasy?)
Call I did, with only laughter
Blown back, as I hurried after;
Till I reached the riverside,

Where I last had seen her glide
In among the reeds, and there
Lost her. But a breath of air
Moved the grass-heads, going by,
And I heard the rushes sigh.

So the chase has always proved;
And Pan never yet has loved,
But the loved one all too soon
Merged in music and was gone, —
Melted like a passing strain,
Vanished like a gust of rain
Or a footfall of the wind,
Leaving not a trace behind.

All that once was Pitys stirs
In the soft voice of the firs.
Lovers, when ye hear that sigh,
Not without a prayer pass by!
And, O lovers, when ye hear,
On a morning soft and clear,
All that once was Echo still
Wandering from hill to hill,
Breathe a prayer lest ye too stray,
Lost upon the mountain way,
And go seeking all your lives
Love, when but his ghost survives!

Then a swaying river reed
From the water, for my need,
In a dream I blindly drew,
Cut and fashioned, ranged and blew, —
Such a music as was played
Never yet since earth was made.
Shrilling, wild and dazed and thin,

All my welling heart therein
Trembled, till the piping grew
Pure as fire and fine as dew,
Till confusion was untangled
From the crowding notes that jangled,
And a new-created world
To my wonder was unfurled,
Sphere by sphere, as climbing sense
Faltered at the imminence
Of the fragile thing called soul
Just beyond oblivion's goal,
And creation's open door

Bade me enter and explore.

Slowly hill and stream and wood
Merged and melted, for my mood,
With the colour of the sun
In the pipe I played upon.
Slowly anger from me fell,
In the coil of that new spell
My own music laid on me,
Like the great rote of the sea,
Like the whisper of the stream,
Like a wood bird's sudden gleam,
Or the gusts that swoop and pass
Through the ripe and seeding grass,—
Perfect rhythm and colour cast
In the perfect mould at last.

Slowly I came back to poise,
A new self with other joys,
Other raptures than before,
Harming less and helping more.
I could strive no more for gain;
Being was my true domain,
And the smiling peace that ever
In the end outruns endeavour.
It was not enough to do;

I must feel, but reason too,
Find the perfect form and fashion
For the elemental passion;
Else must blemish still be hurled
On the beauty of the world, —
Gloom and clang and hate alloy
Colour, melody, and joy,
And the violence of error
Fill the earth with sound and terror.

So I felt the subtle change,
Large, enduring, keen, and strange;
And on that day long ago
I became the god ye know,
Made by music out of man.
Now ye have the pipes of Pan,
Which ye call by Syrinx' name,
Keeping bright a little fame
Few folk ever think upon.
Ah, but where is Syrinx gone?

As the mountain twilight stole
Through the woods from bole to bole,
A dumb warder setting free
Every shy divinity,
I became aware of each
Presence, aspen, bass, and beech;
And they all found voice and made
A green music in the shade.

Therefore, therefore, mortal man,
When ye hear the pipes of Pan,
Marvel not that they should hold
Something sad and calm and old,
Like an eerie minor strain
Running through the strong refrain c
All there is of human woe
Pan has fathomed long ago;
All of sorrow, all of ill,
Kindly Pan remembers still;
Disappointment, grief, disdain,
Stifled impulse and bleak pain,
Pan has learned them; Pan has known
Hurts and passions of his own.

Thus Pan knows the secret hid
Under the Great Pyramid;
Why young lovers for their love
Think the stars are light enough,
And they very well may house
In the odorous fir boughs,
Think there is no light of day
With the loved one gone away,
Use in life, nor pleasure more
By the hearth or out of door, —
Since all things begin and end
But to glad the little friend,
And all gladness is forgot
Where the little friend is not.

Thus Pan melts your human heart
With the magic of his art.
Yet, O heart-distracted man,
When you hear the pipes of Pan,
Marvel not that they should hold
Something sure and strong and bold,
Like a dominant refrain
Heartening the minor strain.

Come into the woods once more;
Leave the fire and close the door;
Trust the spirit that has made
Musical the light and shade,
Still to guard you, still to guide you,
Somewhere in the wood beside you,
Pace for pace upon the road
To your larger next abode.
Though the world should lay a finger
On your arm to bid you linger,
Ye shall neither halt nor tarry

(Little be the load ye carry!)
When ye hear the pipes of Pan
Shrill and pleading in the van.
'Tis the music that has freed you
From the old life, and shall lead you,
Gently wise and strongly fond,
To the greater life beyond.
Yet I whisper to you, "Stay;
That new life is here; to-day
Is your home, whose roof shall rise
From the ground before your eyes."

For Pan loves you and is near,
Though no music you should hear.
Hearken, hearken; it will grow,
Spite of bitterness and woe,
Clear and sweet and undistraught,
(This old earth's impassioned thought,)
And the sorry heart shall learn
What no rapture could discern.

All the music ye have heard:
Mountain brook and orchard bird;
Fifers in the April swamp,
Fiddlers leading August's pomp;
All the mellow flutes of June
Melting on the mating tune;
Pale tree cricket with his bell
Ringing ceaselessly and well,
Sounding silver to the brass
Of his cousin in the grass;
Hot cicada clacking by,
When the air is dusty dry;
Old man owl, with noiseless flight,
Whoo-hoo-hooing in the night;
Surf of ocean, sough of pine;

Note of warbler, sharp and fine;
Rising wind and falling rain,
Lowing cattle on the plain;
And that hardly noticed sound
When the apples come to ground,

On the long, still afternoons,
In the shelter of the dunes;
Chir and guggle, bark and cry,
Bleat, hum, twitter, coo and sigh,
Mew and belling, hoot and bay,
Clack and chirrup, croak and neigh,
Whoof and cackle, whine and creak,
Honk and chatter, caw and squeak;
Wolf and eagle, mink and moose,
Each for his own joyous use
Uttering the heart's desire
As the season bade aspire;
Folk of meadow, crag, and dale,
Open barren and deep swale,
Every diverse rhythm and time
Brought to order, ranged in rhyme:
All these bubbling notes once ran
Thrilling through the pipes of Pan.

Think you Pan forgets the tune
Learned beneath the slim new moon,
When these throbbings all were blent
To the dominant intent?

All the beauties ye have seen:
Autumn scarlet, young spring green;
Floating mists that drift and follow
Up the dark blue mountain hollow;
Yellow sunlight, silver spray;
The wild creatures at their play;
Through still hours the floating seed
Of the thistle and milkweed,
And the purple asters snowed
In a drift beside the road;
Swarthy fern by pebbly shoal;
Mossed and mottled beech-tree bole;
Fireflies in a dewy net,
When the summer eves are wet;
All the bright, gay-coloured things

Buoyed in air on balanced wings;
All earth's wonder; then the sea

In his lone immensity
Only the great stars can share,
And the life uncounted there,
Where the coral gardens lie
And the painted droves go by,
In the water-light and gloom,
Silent till the day of doom:
These have lent, as beauty can,
Colour to the pipes of Pan.

Think you Pan forgets the key
Of their primal melody,
Phrase and motive to revive
Every drooping soul alive?

All the wilding rapture shared
With the loved one, when ye dared
(Lip to lip and knee to knee)
Force the door of destiny,
Greatly loved and greatly gave,
Too divine to stint or save;
All the passion ye have poured
For the joy of the adored,
Spending without thought or measure
Young delight and priceless treasure,
Grown immortal in the hour
When fresh manhood came in flower;

All the ecstasy unpent
From sweet ardours rinding vent
In the coming on of spring,
When the rainy uplands ring,
And the misty woods unfold
To the magic as of old;
All the hot, delicious swoon
Of the teeming summer noon,
When the year is brought to prime
By the bees among the thyme,
And each mortal heart made over

By the wind among the clover:
All these glad things ye shall find
With a free and single mind,
Dreaming eye and cheek of tan,
Lurking in the pipes of Pan.

So the forest wind went by, —
Half a word and half a sigh, —

On a magic night in June,
When the wondrous silent moon
Flooded the blue mountain dove,
And the stream in my beech grove
Uttered secrets strange and deep,
Like one talking in his sleep.

Would ye enter, maid and man,
The novitiate of Pan?
Know the secret of the strain
Lures you through the summer plain,
Guess the meaning of the thrill
Haunts you on the autumn hill?
Would ye too contrive a measure
Out of love, to fill your leisure?
Learn to fashion a flute-reed
That should answer to love's need,
When the spirit in you cries
To be given form and guise
Others may perceive and love,
Fair and much accounted of, —
Craves to be the tenant heart
In some wild, new, lovely art,
Such as haunts the glades of spring
When the woodlands bloom and ring?

While the silver night still broods
On the mountain solitudes,
And the great white planet still
Is undimmed upon the hill,
Ere a hint of subtile change
Steals across the purple range

To arouse the sleeping bird, —
Hear the wise old master's word,
When he leads the pregnant notes
From the reedy golden throats,
And the traveller, in their spell,
Halts, and wonders what they tell!

Here is Pan's green flower, the earth,
He has tended without dearth,
Brought to blossom, fruit, and seed
By the sap's imperious need,
When the season of the sun
Sets its fervour free to run.
Sap of tree and pith of man,
Ah, but they are dear to Pan!

Not a creature stirs or moves,
But Pan heartens and approves;
Not a being loves or dies,
But Pan knows the sacrifice.
Man or stripling, wife or maid,

Pan is ever by to aid;
And no harm can come to you,
But his great heart feels it, too.

Love's use let the joiner prove
By the fit of tongue and groove;
Or the smith, whose forge's play
Stubborn metal must obey;
Let the temple-builders own,
As they mortise stone to stone;
Or the sailor, when he reeves
Sheet and halliard through the sheaves;
Or the potter, from whose wheel
Fair and finished shapes upsteal,
As by magic of command,
Guided by the loving hand.

Ye behold in love the tether
Binding the great world together;
For without that coil of wonder
The round world would fall asunder,
And your hearts be filled with sadness
At a great god's seeming madness,
Where they now have peace, and hope,
Somewhere, somehow, time will ope,
And the loneliness be sated,
And the longing be abated
In the loved one, lovely past
All imagining at last,
Melting, fragrant, starry-eyed,
Like a garden in its pride,
Odorous with hint and rapture
Of soft joys no word can capture.

Ah, the sweet Pandean strain!
He who hears it once shall gain
Freedom of the open door,
Willing to go back no more.

When ye hear the sea pipes thunder,
Bow the loving heart in wonder;
When ye hear the wood pipes play,

Lift the door latch and away;
When ye hear the hill pipes calling,
Where the pure cold brooks are falling,
Follow till your feet have found
The desired forgotten ground,
And ye know, past all unlearning,
By the raptured quench of yearning,
What the breath is to the reed
Whence the magic notes are freed,
What new life the gods discover
To the loved one and the lover,
When their fabled dreams come true
In the wondrous fair and new.

For the music of the earth,
Helping joy-of-heart to birth,
(Field note, wood note, wild or mellow,

Bidding all things fare and fellow,)
Means that wisdom lurks behind
The enchantment of the mind;
And your longing keen and tense
Still must trust the lead of sense,
Hint of colour, form, and sound,
Till it reach the perfect round,
And completed blend its strain
With the haunted pipes again.
Ye must learn the lift and thrill
That elate the wood pipes still;
Feel the ecstasy and shiver
Of the reed notes in the river;
Shudder to the minor trace
In the sea's eternal bass,
And give back the whole heart's treasure
To supreme the music's measure,
Glad that love should sink and sound
All the beauty in earth's bound.

All this loveliness which ran
Searching through the pipes of Pan,—
All this love must merge and blend
With Pan's piping in the end.
All the knowledge ye draw near
At the ripening of the year,
Living one day at a time,
Innocent of fear or crime,
(When the mountain slopes put on
Their brave scarlet in the sun,

When the sea assumes a blue
Such as April never knew,
And the marshes, fields, and skies
Sing with colour as day dies,)
Peaceful, undistracted, free,
In your earth-born piety;
All the love when friend for friend
Dared misfortune to the end, —
Fronted failure, flouted harm,
For the sake of folding arm, —

Bravelier trod the earth, and bolder,
For the touch of hand on shoulder;
All the homely smiles and tears
Ever given childish years;
Every open, generous deed
Lending help to human need;
Every kindliness to age,
Every impulse true and sage,
Lifting concord out of strife,
Bringing beauty into life:
These no feeble faith can ban
Ever from the pipes of Pan.

Think you Pan forgets the scheme
Or the cadence of his theme?
Ah, your wit must still discover
No mere madness of a lover,
Headstrong, whimsical, and blind,
But a prompting sane and kind,
Scope and purpose, hint and plan,

Lurking in the pipes of Pan;
Calling ever, smooth and clear,
Courage to the heeding ear;
Fluting ever, sweet and high,
Wisdom to the passer-by;
Sounding ever, soft and far,
Happiness no grief can mar.

This enchantment Pan bequeaths
Unto every lip that breathes;
Cunning unto every hand
Agile under will's command;
Unto every human heart
The inheritance of art,
Lighted only by a gleam
Of the dear and deathless dream, —

Power out of hurt and stain
To bring beauty back again,
And life's loveliness restore
To a toiling age once more.

Yes, the world is growing old,
But the joys it used to hold,
Love and beauty, only grow
Greater as they come and go,
Larger, keener, and more splendid,
Seen to be superbly blended,
As the cadenced years go by,
Into chord and melody,
Strong and clear as ever ran
Over the rude pipes of Pan.

So the music passed and died
In the dark green mountain side
The entranced ravine took on
A new purple, faint and wan;
And I heard across the hush
A far solitary thrush
From the hemlocks deep and still
Fluting day upon the bill.

MARSYAS

In Celaenae by Meander lived a youth once long ago
And one passion great and splendid brimmed his heart to overflow,
Filled the world for him with beauty, sense and colour, joy and glow.

Not ambition and not power, love nor luxury nor fame,
Beckoned him to join their pageant, summoned Marsyas by name,
Bidding unreluctant spirit dare to keep the soaring aim;

But the sorceries of music, note and rapture, tone and thrill,
Sounding the serene enchantment over meadow, stream and hill,
Blew for him the undesisting magic call-note, followed still.

And he followed. Heart of wonder, how the keen blue smoke upcurled
From the shepherd huts to heaven! How the dew lay silver-pearled
Where sleek sided cattle wandered through the morning of the world!

On a stream bank lay the idler dreaming dreams for it was Spring
And he heard the frogs in chorus make the watery marshes ring;
Heard new comers at their nesting in the vineyards pipe and sing;

Heard the river lisp below him; heard the wind chafe reed on reed;
Every earth-imprisoned creature rinding vent and voice at need.
Ah! if only so could mortal longing and delight be freed!

Hark! What piercing unknown cry comes stealing o'er the forest ground,
Pouring sense and soul together in an ecstasy new-found?
Dream's fulfilment brought to pass and life untethered at a bound!

Then it pauses, and the youth beyond the river-bend perceives
A divine one in her beauty stand, half-hidden by the leaves,
Fingering a wondrous wood-pipe, whence the clear sound joys or grieves.

As he looked, entranced and musing at the marvel of the strain,
All her loveliness uncinctured with a madness touched his brain,
And love, like a vernal fever, dyed him with its scarlet stain.

But Athene, glancing downward in the silver of the stream,
As she fluted, saw her perfect mouth distorted by a seam;
Faltered, stopped, and, disconcerted, seemed to ponder half in dream

For a rueful moment; and then with reluctance tossed the reed
She had fashioned in a happy leisure mood to serve her need
Back into the tranquil river, nothing but a river weed,

All the cunning life that filled it quenched and spilt and flung away,
To go seaward to oblivion on a wandering stream. But stay!
The young Phrygian lad has seen it, marked the current set his way,

Stooped and picked it from the water; put the treasure-trove to lip;
Blown his first breath, faint yet daring; felt the wild notes crowd and slip
Into melody and meaning from each testing finger-tip.

Then, ah, then had mortal spirit sweep and room at last to range
The lost limits of creation and the borderlands of change,
All earth's loveliness transmuting into something new and strange;

All of beauty, all of knowledge, all of wonder, fused and caught
In the rhythmus of the music, weaving out of sense and thought
And a touch of love the fabric out of which the world was wrought.

And the joy of each new cadence, as the glad notes pressed and cried,
Eager for the strain's fulfilment, as they rose and merged and died
In the music's utmost measure, filled the rose-grey mountain side,

Touched the sheep-bells in the meadow, moved the rushes in the stream,
And suffused the youth with glory as he passed from theme to theme;
Made him as the gods of morning in the ampler air of dream.

Ah, what secret, what enchantment so could help the human need,
Save the breath of life that lingered in the hollow of the reed,
Since the careless mouth of beauty blessed it with so little heed?

There he stood, a youth transfigured in the young world's golden glow.
Made immortal in a moment by the music's melting flow,
Pattern of the artist's glory for the after years to know.

There he stands for us in picture, with the pipe whereon he plays;
The slow, large-eyed cattle wonder, and the flocks forget to graze,
While upon the hill a shepherd turns and listens in amaze.

In the woods the timid creatures, reassured, approach and peer,
Half aware the charm's allurement they must follow as they hear
Is the first far-looked-for presage of the banishment of fear.

Silence falls upon the woodland, quiet settles on the plain;
Earth and air and the blue heaven, without harm or taint or stain,
Are restored to their old guise of large serenity again.

Thus the player at his piping in the early mode and grave
Took from Wisdom the inventress what the earth in bounty gave,
And therein to round completion put the beating heart and brave.

So, you artists and musicians, earth awaits perfection still;
Wisdom tarries by the brookside, beauty loiters on the hill,
For the love that shall reveal them with the yet undreamed-of skill.

Love be therefore all your passion, the one ardour that ye spend
To enhance the craft's achievement with significance and trend,
Making faultless the wild strain that else were faulty to the end.

Love must lend the magic cadence that un-earthly dying fall
When the simple sweet earth-music takes us captive past recall,
And the loved one and the lover lose this world, nor care at all.

SYRINX

Once I saw (O breath of Summer!) in the azure prime of June,
When the Northland takes her joy and sets her wintered life in tune,
The soft wind come down the river, where a heron slept at noon;

Stir the ripening meadow-grasses, lift the lily-pads, and stray
Through the tall green ranks of rushes bowing to its ghostly sway;
Then I heard it, like a whisper of the world, take voice and say:

"Mortal by the wood-wind's murmur and the whisper of the stream,
I, who am the breath of grasses and the soul of Summer's dream,
Once was Syrinx, whom a great god loved and lost and made the theme

"Of his mournful minor music. Nay, I who had worn the guise
Which allured him, yet eluded, vanishing before his eyes,
When his heart held lonely commune, taking counsel to devise

"Some new solace for sad lovers that should give the spirit vent,
Lovelier than speech of mortals where the stricken soul is pent
And the longing gropes for language large enough for beauty's bent;

"When he drew the reeds and ranged them, rank by rank from low to shrill,
Bound them with the flax together I was inspiration still,
I was heartache crying through them, I was echo on the hill.

"And forever I am cadence, joyous, welling, sad or fond,
When the breath of god or mortal, breaking time's primeval bond,
Blows upon the mouths of wood and all the mellow throats respond.

"Not a flute, but I have hidden in its haunted hollow mould;
In the deep Sicilian twilight, when the shepherd piped to fold,
I have been the eerie calling of the Pan pipes rude and old;

"From the ivory monaulos, when the soft Egyptian stars
Sentried Cleopatra's gardens, through the open window-bars
I went forth, a splendid torment, o'er the dreaming nenuphars.

"In the silver-mounted laurel played by some Byzantine boy,
I was frenzy, when the throng night after night went mad for joy,
As the dancer Theodora made the Emperor her toy.

"In the boxwood bound with gold I drew my captives down the Nile,
To the love-feasts of Bubastis, lovers by the thousand file,
Willing converts to my love-call, children of the changeless smile.

"Babylonian Mylitta heard me keep the limpid tune,
When the lovers danced before her at the feast of the new moon,
Till the rosy flowers of beauty through her sacred groves were strewn.

"And Sidonian Astarte and the Asian Cypriote
Knew the large unhurried measure of my earth-sweet pagan rote,
When the dancing youths before them followed me from note to note.

"Where some lithe Bithynian flute-boy, nude and golden in the sun,
Set his red mouth to the twin pipes, I was in each pause and run,
When his manhood took the meaning of the love-notes one by one.

"And amid the fields of iris by the blue Ionian sea,
I was solemn-hearted sweetness and pure passion soon to be
In the dark-haired little maid who piped her budding melody.

"I was youth and love and rapture, I was madness in their veins,
Calling through the heats of Summer, calling in the soft Spring rains,
From the olive Phrygian hillsides and the deep Boeotian plains.

"I but blew, and mortals followed; I but breathed, and they were glad,—
King and mendicant and sailor, courtesan and shepherd lad;
For there is no creed nor canon laid on music's myriad.

"Not a tribe nor race nor people born in darkest savagery,
Dwellers in the Afric forest or the islands of the sea,
But I wooed them from their war-drums — made them gentle — set them free.

"Silence fell upon the tam-tams throbbing terror through the night,
And the prayer-gongs ceased to conjure cowering villages with fright,
When my cool note, clear as morning, called them to a new delight.

"I, the breath of flute and oboe, golden wood and silver reed,
Put away their fear, and taught them with my love-tone to give heed,
When the love grew large within them, to the lovely spirit's need.

"Henceforth no mere frantic rhythm of beating foot and patting hand,
Nor monotonous marimba could suffice for soul's demand,
When Joy called her wayworn children and Peace wandered through the land.

"Love must build a better music than the strumming tambourine,
To ensphere his worlds of wonder, height and depth and space between,
Pleasure-lands for Soul, the lover, to preempt as his demesne.

"So he took the simple reed-note, as a dewdrop clear and round,
Blew it (magic of creation!) to the tenuous profound
Of sheer gladness, light and colour of the universe of sound.

"And there soars the shining structure, tone on tone as star on star,
Spheres of knowledge and of beauty, where love's compensations are,
And the plenitudes of spirit move to rhythm without a jar;

"Every impulse in its orbit swinging to the utmost range
Of the normal sweep of being, through unfathomed gulfs of change,
Poised, unswerved, and never finding aught unlovely or unstrange.

"When some dark Peruvian lover set the love-flute to his lip,
I was the new soft enchantment loosed upon the dusk, to slip
Through the trees and thrill the loved one from warm nape to finger-tip;

"Till she could not choose but follow where my player piped for her;
So I roused the love within her, set the gipsy pulse astir,
With my wild delicious pleading, strong as incense, fine as myrrh.

"When for love the Winnebago took his courting-flute and played
His wild theme for days together near the lodge-door of his maid,
I was ritual and rapture of the triumph he essayed.

"And my brown Malayan lovers pierce the living gold bamboo,
For the lone melodious accents of the wind to wander through,
While my haunting spirit tells them many a secret old and true.

"In the soft Sumatran pan-flute with its seven notes I plead;
I am help to the Marquesan in his slender scarlet reed;
From the immemorial East I draw my dark-eyed gipsy breed.

"Chukma, Dyak, Mahalaka, Papuan and Ashanti,
Hillmen from the Indian snows, canoemen from the Carib sea,
Tribesmen from the world's twelve corners, at my whisper come to me

"All the garlanded earth-children in their gala bright array,
Laughing like the leaves, or sighing like the grass-heads which I sway;
For my lure is swift to lead them, and my solace strong to stay.

"And the road must melt before them and their piping fill all lands,
Till a new world at their fluting like a magic flower expands,
And Soul's unexplored dominion is surrendered to their hands.

"Did not I, the wood-breath, calling, make thy mortal pulses ring,
And thy many-seasoned roof-tree with its dusty rafters sing?
Was not I the long sweet love-throb in the music-house of Spring?

"Think how all the golden willows and the maples crimson-keyed,
Kept the rare appointed season, flowering at the instant need,
When the wood-pipes gave my summons and the marshy flutes were freed!

"Love be, then, in every heart-beat, when the year comes round to June,
And life reaches up to rapture, lingering on the perfect tune,
As this evening in your valley silvered by the early moon."

Thus I heard the voice of Syrinx, by the dreamy river shore,
Sift and cease, as one might pass through a large room and close the door;
And I knew myself a stranger on this lovely earth no more.

THE MAGIC FLUTE

Hear, O Syrinx, thou lost dryad! Marsyas, thou mortal, hear!
If to lovely and free spirits it is granted to draw near
And revisit the whole earth from some far-off and twilight sphere,

Like the limpid star of evening hanging o'er the ark hill brow,
Globed in light to touch this valley where a worshipper I bow,
O give heed, and of your wisdom help a mortal over now!

Lend him, novice at your flute-work, learner of the magic cry,
Something, howsoever faulty, of that cunning ecstasy,
The inevitable cadence where the raptures pause and die,

You could marshal at your bidding from the wind-blown river reeds,
Mark to rhythm and mould to beauty, plastic for perfection's needs;
Skill to give the spirit lodgment where the longing fancy leads!

Souls of lovers lost in music! You who were beloved of Pan,
Piping madness through the meadow where the silver river ran,
You who, favoured of Athene, found her careless gift to man,

O stray hither, and recalling some such earth-born golden hour,
When the thrushes eased their sorrow, and the laurel was in flower,
Give this last lost child of nature one least pittance of your power!

So he shall be well accounted love's own minstrel first and best,
By another shy wild Syrinx when he puts the gift to test,
For a single day immortal. And the gods make good the rest!

Hear, sweetheart, the lonely thrushes! Pure and pleading up the clove,
From the dark moon-haunted hemlocks and the spacious dim beech grove,
Pierced by love's own silver planet with a path for us to rove,

Comes the rapture, clear, unsullied, undistracted, undismayed,
Heart of earth that still remembers how her strength and joy were made,
When the breath of life was given and the touch of doom was stayed,

The great joyance of creation welling through the world once more;
Love in power and pride and passion, crying still at beauty's door;
Soul in contemplation ranging the star-lighted forest floor.

Once . . . O little girl, lift up that dear, wild, tender wood-nymph's face
To your lover's who so loves you, gladdening all this leafy place,
Where as music merged in moonshine sense and spirit interlace!

In the first of time was Hathor, the Egyptian Ashtoreth,
She who bore the mighty Sun and quickened nature with her breath,
Rocked the cradle of the Nile and gave men life and gave them death.

Once to share her mysteries, when earth grew green with spring, there came
To her temple in Bubastis, needy and unknown to fame,
A young herdsman golden-haired and tall, Argalioth by name.

And his undeflowered beauty, fair as lotus, slim as palm,
With his voice like sweet hill-water sounding in the choric psalm,
Touched the mighty heart there brooding in inviolable calm.

And a sigh as of the wind arose; the song was hushed; the veil
Of the Shrine, which none might enter, moved and shimmered like a sail,
Or the golden boreal lights that hang across our Northern trail.

In astonishment the dancers halted. Then the voice said "Peace!
Let my son Argalioth come near. It is a gift of peace.
Henceforth only truth and goodness, finding virtue, shall find peace."

Then the lad arose and went behind the veil, and all was still.
Slowly, as from out all distance, rising far and fine and shrill,
Came a flute-note, strong as sea-wind, clear as morning on the hill,

Grew and gained and swelled and triumphed, lingering from tone to tone,
Golden deep to silver treble, pure and passionate and lone,
Marking time to things eternal, touching bounds of spirit's zone,

Filling all the space between with all the wonder and despair
Reach and compass and fulfilment soul could ever dream or dare
Of the bliss beyond all telling, when the wild sense grows aware.

Then before those spellbound watchers from the Holy Place returned
The youth, girt in scarlet linen, with a countenance where burned
The great glory of his vision and the secret he had learned.

In his hand a yellow flute-reed bound with seven silver bands;
From brown foot to red-gold hair a figure that might haunt all lands
With distraction and enthralment, while this earth in beauty stands.

Not a word he spoke; serenely trod the marble to the door;
Set the flute to mouth, and piping strains no ear had heard before,
Passed out through the golden weather, and no man beheld him more.

Yet there lingered, ah, what music! Not a listener in that throng,
Through the years that came upon him, but at times would hear the long
Piercing and melodious cadence, summer-sweet and autumn-strong,

Heard so long ago; and always, as if musing, he would say,
"It is Hathor's magic flute. In some blue valley far away,
By a well among the palms her wanderer has paused to play!"

For through all the earth he wandered with his magic pipe; and none
Heard that piping, but they straightway knew that their old life was done,
And the glamour was upon them, prudence lost and freedom won.

He it was who touched with madness, soft sweet madness of the spring,
The green-throated frogs, whose chorus makes the grassy meadows ring,
And the birds who come with April, and must break their heart or sing;

Touched his fellow mortals even with a madness of the mind,
Till they, too, must rise and follow, leaving sober tasks behind,
While a thing called love possessed them with a craving sweet and blind,

And they knew no fear thereafter, save the one supreme despair,
Having loved, to lose the loved one, the one lovely friend could share
The vast loneliness of being. What mute bitterness were there!

And we all are Hathor's children, brothers of the frogs and birds,
Who have listened once forever to the pipe whose magic words
None can fathom, though we follow dumbly as the flocks and herds.

Thenceforth howsoe'er we wander, all our care is but to know
Truth, the Sorceress whose spell of beauty can entrance us so,
As it was with happy lovers in their wisdom long ago.

And to all men once a lifetime comes that music sweet and shrill,
Pleading for the life's perfection, good's preferment over ill,
Beauty's issue from debasement, the deliverance of will.

Many hear it not, or hearing turn with heedless hearts away,
Or their soul is deaf with greed or lust or anger or dismay,
And the precious fateful moment passes. But the wise are they,

Who preserve without disquiet the serene and open mind,
The impassioned poise of spirit, lodged in senses more refined
Than the quaking aspen breathed on by the unseen secret wind.

So in spite of tears and turmoil many a radiant hour they know,
Hearing o'er the roofs of men the far off magic woodpipes blow,
With a message for the morrow bidding them arise and go.

And that message? What I cherish most, this sweet white night of June,
When from sheath of fragrant lace-work slips one shoulder, like the moon
From the pine-tops with a lustre such as made its lover swoon.

Once on Latmus; when your hair falls, like a vine the stars peep through;
When I kiss your heart out, much as mighty Pan the reed-pith drew,

And your breath in one " Beloved! " answers like the reed he blew;

What I prize most, and most treasure, is this knowledge great and sure:
He who knows love, knows the secret, he who has love has the lure,
Of the strain whereto this earth was moulded well and must endure.

Hush, ah, hush! Lie still! The music is not yet gone from the firs,
Haply here the Ancient Mother, in this solitude of hers,
Where the mighty veil of silence, leaves and stars, the hill-wind stirs,

Some new larger revelation would vouchsafe to you and me
Of the sorceries of summer or the secret of the sea,
Whose sheer beauty shall enthral us while its truth shall set us free.

O my golden Syrinx, surely we have heard the magic flute,
Whose dark wild mysterious transport in a moment can transmute
All the heart and life forever, making spirits that were mute

Musical and glad! And we have listened to that lost flute-strain,
Whose long sweet and sobbing minor is the record of the rain,
Whose proud passion is the gladness when the spring comes back again.

Hark, the thrushes at their fluting! The old wizardry and stress
Of entrancement are upon them, Wise ones of the wilderness,
Who can say but they have burdens of a joy beyond our guess?

Long since did the magic minstrel take them silent from the bough
In his hands, and with the secret breath of life their throats endow,
As this rose-red mouth of beauty burning meward I do now!

A SHEPHERD IN LESBOS

All night long my cabin roof resounded
With the mighty 'murmur of the rain;
All night long I heard the silver cohorts
Tramping down the valley to the plain;

All night long the ringing rain-drops volleyed
On the hollow drum-heads of the leaves
In a wild tattoo, while gusty hill-winds
Fifed The Young Pans' March about the eaves.

So all night within the mountain forest
Passed the shadowy forces at review;
And they bore me back to time's beginning
When the wonder of the world was new.

Then from out the gloom there came a vision
Of the beauty of the earth of old,
The unclouded face and gracious figure,
Filleted with laurel and green-stoled,

Such as Daphne wore the day she wandered
Through the silent beech-wood of the god,
When a sunray through the roof of shadows
Wheeled and stole behind her where she trod, —

When the loveliness of earth, transfigured
By one touch of rapture, grew divine,
Ere it fled before the unveiled presence
To indwell forever its green shrine.

Like a mist I saw the hair's gold glory,
The grave eyes, the childish scarlet lip,
And the rose-pink fervour that afforded
Soul the sheath to fill from tip to tip.

On her mouth she laid a warning finger,
And her slow calm enigmatic smile
Told me, ere she spoke, one-half the message;
Then I heard (my heart stood still the while),

"Mortal, wouldst thou know the maddening transport
No mere earth-born lover may attain,
Till some woodland deity hath loved him,
And her beauty mounted to his brain?

"Thenceforth he becomes, with her for mistress,
Master of the moods and minds of men,
Moulding as he will their deeds and daring,
All their follies open to his ken;

"Yet is he a wanderer forever,
Without respite seeking the unknown.
Wouldst thou leave the world for one who offers
But the beauty bounded by her zone?"

When I woke in golden morning dyeing
The dark valley and the purple hill,
Flushing at the doorway of the forest,
Flowered my mountain laurel, cool and still.

How I chose? Have ye not heard in Lesbos
Of a mad young shepherd by the shore,

Whose wild piping bids the traveller tarry
Some immortal sorrow to deplore?

On a morning by the river marges
Many a passer-by hath heard that strain,
Sweet and sad and strange and full of longing
As a bird-note through the purple rain.

In a maze the haunted music holds them
With its meaning past all guess or care;
With its magic note the lonely cadence
Swells and sinks and dies upon the air;

And they say, "It is the stricken shepherd
Whom the nymph's enchantment set astray,
And the spell of his bewildering vision
Holds him fast a lover from that day.

"His dark theme no mortal may interpret;
But forever when the wood-pipes blow,
Some remembered and mysterious echo
Calls us unresisting and we go."

DAPHNE

I know that face!
In some lone forest place,
When June brings back the laurel to the hills,
Where shade and sunlight lace,

Where all day long
The brown birds make their song
A music that seems never to have known
Dismay nor haste nor wrong

I once before
Have seen thee by the shore,
As if about to shed the flowery guise
And be thyself once more.

Dear, shy, soft face,
With just the elfin trace
That lends thy human beauty the last touch
Of wild, elusive grace!

Can it be true,

A god did once pursue
Thy gleaming beauty through the glimmering wood,
Drenched in the Dorian dew,

Too mad to stay
His hot and headstrong way,
Demented by the fragrance of thy flight,
Heedless of thy dismay?

But I to thee
More gently fond would be,
Nor less a lover woo thee with soft words
And woodland melody;

Take pipe and play
Each forest fear away;
Win thee to idle in the leafy shade
All the long Summer day;

Tell thee old tales
Of love, that still avails
More than all mighty things in this great world,
Still wonderworks nor fails;

Teach thee new lore,
How to love more and more,
And find the magical delirium
In joys unguessed before.

I would try over
And over to discover
Some wild, sweet, foolish, irresistible
New way to be thy lover —

New, wondrous ways
To fill thy golden days,
Thy lovely pagan body with delight,
Thy loving heart with praise.

For I would learn,
Deep in the brookside fern,
The magic of the syrinx whispering low
With bubbly fall and turn;

Mock every note
Of the green woodbird's throat,
Till some wild strain, impassioned yet serene,
Should form and float

Far through the hills,
Where mellow sunlight fills
The world with joy, and from the purple vines
The brew of life distils.

Ah, then indeed
Thy heart should have no need
To tremble at a footfall in the brake,
And bid thy bright limbs speed.

But night would come,
And I should make thy home
In the deep pines, lit by a yellow star
Hung in the dark blue dome

A fragrant house
Of woven balsam boughs,
Where the great Cyprian mother should receive
Our warm unsullied vows.

THE LOST DRYAD

Where are you gone from the forest,
Leaving the mountain-side lonely
And all the beech woods deserted,
O my dear Daphne?

All the day long I go seeking
Trace of your flowerlike footprint.
Will not the dew on the meadow
Tell tale of Daphne?

Will not the sand on the sea-shore
Treasure that magical impress
For the disconsolate longing
Lover of Daphne?

Will not the moss and the fern-bed
Bearing the mould of her beauty,
Tell me where wandered and rested
Rose-golden Daphne?

All the night through I go hearkening
Every wild murmurous echo,
Hint of your laughter, the birdlike

Voice of my Daphne.

Why do the poplar leaves whisper
Things to themselves in the silence,
Though no wind visits the valley,
Daphne, my Daphne?

Listen! I hear their small voices,
An elfin multitude, mingle,
Lisping in silver-leaf language,
"Daphne, O Daphne!"

Listen! I hear the cold hill-brook
Plash down the clove on its pebbles,
And the ravine drenched in moonlight
Echoing, "Daphne!"

"Daphne," the rain says at nightfall;
"Daphne," the wind breathes at morning;
And a voice troubles the hot noon
Uttering "Daphne."

Ah, what impassioned remembrance,
In the dark pines in the starlight,
Touches the dream of your wood-thrush,
O my lost Daphne,

Dyeing his sleep like a bubble
Coloured for joy, and the note comes,
Golden, enchanted, eternal,
Calling for Daphne!

O Mother Earth, at how many
Thresholds of lone-dwelling mortals
Must I, a wayfarer, tarry,
Asking for Daphne?

How many times see their faces
Fade to incredulous wonder,
Hearing in some remote vale
The story of Daphne,

Ere I at last through the twilight
Hear the soft rapturous outcry,
And as of old there will greet me
Far-wandered Daphne?

THE DEAD FAUN

Who hath done this thing? What wonder is this that lies
On the green earth so still under purple skies,
Like a hyacinth shaft the careless mower has cut
And thought of no more ?

Who hath wrought this pitiful wrong on the lovely earth?
What ruthless hand could ruin that harmless mirth?
O heart of things, what undoing is here, never now
To be mended more!

No more, O beautiful boy, shall thy fleet feet stray
Through the cool beech wood on the shadowy mountain way,
Nor halt by the well at noon, nor trample the flowers
On the forest floor.

Thy beautiful light-seeing gold-green eyes, so glad
When day came over the hill, so wondrous sad
When the burning sun went slowly under the sea,
Shall look no more.

Thy nimble fingers that plucked the fruit from the bough,
Or fondled the nymph's bright hair and filleted brow,
Or played the wild mellow pipe of thy father Pan,
Shall play no more.

Thy sensitive ears that knew all the speech of the wood,
Every call of the birds and the creatures, and understood
What the wind to the water said, what the river replied,
Shall hear no more.

Thy scarlet and lovely mouth which the dryads knew,
Dear whimsical ardent mouth that love spoke through,
For all the kisses of life that it took and gave,
Shall say no more.

Who hath trammelled those feet that never again shall rove?
Who hath bound these hands that never again shall move?
Who hath quenched the lamp in those eyes that never again
Shall be lighted more?

Who hath stopped those ears from our heart-broken words forever?
Who hath sealed that wonderful mouth with its secret forever?
Who hath touched this innocent being with pitiless death,
And he is no more?

He was fair as a mortal and spiritual as a flower;
He knew no hate, but was happy within the hour.
The Gods had given him beauty and freedom and joy,
Could they give no more?

Is all their wisdom and power so fond a thing?
Must he perish, nor ever return with returning Spring,
But be left like a dead-ripe fruit on the ground for a stranger
To find and deplore?

They have given to mortal man the immortal scope,
The perilous chance, unrest and remembrance and hope,
That imperfection may come to perfection still
By some fabled shore.

Did they give this being, this marvellous work of their hands,
No breath of the greater life with its grief and demands?
Do beauty and love without bitter knowledge attain
This and no more?

The wind may whisper to him, he will heed no more;
The leaves may murmur and lisp, he will laugh no more;
The oreads weep and be heavy at heart for him,
He will care no more.

The reverberant thrushes may peal from the hemlock glooms,
The summer clouds be woven on azure looms ;
He is done with all lovely things of earth forever
And ever more.

HYLAS

Cool were the grey-mottled beeches,
Quiet with noon were the fern-beds,
Where by the bubbling spring water
Tarried young Hylas.

Whistling a song of the rowers,
Dipping his jar till it gurgled,
Suddenly there the bright naiads
(Woe for thee, Hylas!)

Looked and beheld his fair beauty
Better their well-head, and straightway
Exquisite longing possessed them
Only for Hylas.

When he returned not at sundown,
"Over long," said his companions,
As slow dismay came upon them,
"Tarries young Hylas."

Never again did his comrades
Find the lost rower, nor maidens
See from their doorways at twilight
Home-coming Hylas.

Thenceforth another must labour
To the timed thud of his rowlock,
And only legends keep tally
Of the lost Hylas.

Yet even now, when the springtime
Verdures the valley, and rain-winds
Voyage for lands undiscovered,
As once did Hylas,

With a great star on the hill-crest
In purple evening, a flute-note
Pierces the dusk, and a voice calls,
"Hylas, Hylas!"

AT PHÆDRA'S TOMB

What old grey ruin can this be,
Beside the blue Saronic Sea?
What tomb is this, what temple here,
Thus side by side so many a year?

This is that temple Phædra built
To Aphrodite, having spilt
Her whole heart's great warm love in vain,
One lovely mortal's love to gain;
Yet trusting by that fervent will,
Consuming and unconquered still,
In spite of failure and of fate,
By favour of the gods to sate
Her splendid lost imperious
Mad love for young Hippolytus,
Whose brilliant beauty seemed to glow
Like a tall Alp in rosy snow,
While love and passion, wind and fire,

Flared through the field of her desire.

"Great Mother, come from Paphos now
With benediction on thy brow,
And pity! Not beneath the sun
Lives such another hapless one.
O Aphrodite of the sea,
For love have mercy upon me!
Give me his beauty now to slake
This body's longing and soul's ache!
Touch his cold heart until he know
The divine sorrow of love's woe."

What madness hers, what folly his!
And all their beauty come to this
Epitome of mortal doom —
A name, a story, and a tomb!

Have ye not seen the fog from sea
On Autumn mornings silently
Steal in to land, and wrap the sun
With its grey, cold oblivion?

The goddess would not smile on her,
On him no gentler mood confer.
He still must flush his maiden whim;
She still must leash her love for him,
A fancy lawless and superb,
Too wild to tame, too strong to curb,
Too great for her to swerve or stay
In our half-hearted modern way.

Have ye not seen the fog from land
Blow out to sea, and leave the band
Of orange marsh and lilac shore
To brood in Autumn peace once more?

So there survives the magic fame
Of her imperishable name,
Light from a time when love was great,
And strong hearts had no fear of fate,
But lived and strove and wrought and died,
With beauty for their only guide.

And yet this temple, raised and wrought
With prayers and tears, availed her naught.
The years with it have had their will;
Her soft name is a by-word stiil

For thwarted spirit, vexed and teased
By yearnings that cannot be eased,
The soul that chafes upon the mesh
Of tenuous yet galling flesh.

How blue that midday shadow is
In the white dust of Argolis! . . .
This is her tomb. . . . See, near at hand,
This myrtle! Here she used to stand
Those days when her love-haunted eyes
Saw her new-builded hope arise,
Watching the masons set the stone
And fingering her jewelled zone,
Or moving restless to and fro,
Her pale brows knit a little, so.

Look! every leaf pierced through and through!
I doubt not the gold pin she drew
From her dark hair, and, as the storm
Of love swept through her lovely form
With pique and passion, thrust on thrust,
Vented her vehemence. O dust,
That once entempled such a flame
With beauty, colour, line and name,
And gave great Love a dwelling-place
Behind so fair, so sad a face,
Where is thy wilful day-dream now,
That passionate lip, that moody brow?

Ah, fair Greek woman, if there bloom
Some flower of knowledge in the gloom,
Receive the piteous, loving sigh
Of one more luckless passer-by.
Peace, peace, wild heart! Unsatisfied
Has every mortal lived and died,
Since thy dear beauty found a bed
Forever with the dreaming dead,
In seagirt Hellas long ago,
Immortal for thy mortal woe!

A YOUNG PAN'S PRAYER

O pipes of Pan,
Make me a man,
As only your piercing music can!
When I set my lip

To your reedy lip,
And you feel the urging man-breath slip

Through fibre and flake,
Bidding you wake
To the strange new being for beauty's sake,
I pray there be
Returned to me
The strength of the hills and the strength of the sea.

O river reed,
In whom the need
Of the journeying river once was freed,
As of old your will
Was the water's will,
To quiver and call or sleep and be still,

So now anew
I breathe in you
The ardour no alchemy can subdue,
And add the dream, —
The immortal gleam
That never yet fell on meadow or stream.

I breathe and blow
On your dumb mouth so,
Till your lurking soul is alive and aglow.
Ah, breathe in me
The strength of the sea,
The calm of the hills and the strength of the sea!

Love, joy, and fear,
From my faint heart here,
Shall melt in your cadence wild and clear.
With freedom and hope
I range and grope,
Till I find new stops in your earthly scope.

The pleading strain
Of pathos and pain,
The diminished chord and the lost refrain;
The piercing sigh,
The joyous cry,
The sense of what shall be bye and bye;

The grief untold
Out of man's heart old,
Which endures that another may still be bold

The wiser will
That foregoes self-will
And aspires to truth beyond trammel or ill;

Ambition unsure,
And the splendid lure
Of whim in his harlequin vestiture;
And the reach of sound
Into thought's profound;
All these I add to your power earth-bound;

But most, the awe
That perceives where law
Is revealed at last without fault or flaw, —
The touch of mind
That would search and find
The measure of beauty, the purpose of kind.

So with the fire
Of man's desire
Your notes shall outreach the mountain choir.
Brook, breeze, and bird
Shall hear the Word,
And know 'tis their master they have heard.

And the lowly reed,
Whose only need
Was to sigh with the wind in the river weed,
Shall be heard as far
As from star to star,
Where Algol answers to Algebar.

For the soul must trace
Her wondrous race
By a seventh sense on the charts of space,
Till she come at last,
Through the vague and vast,
To her own heart's haven fixed and fast.

Opipes of Pan,
Whose music ran
Through the world ere ever my age began.
When I set my lip
To your woodland lip,
I pray some draft of your virtue slip

From each mellow throat,
As note by note,

A learner, I try for the secret rote,
The rhythm and theme
That shall blend man's dream
Of perfection with nature's imperfect scheme!

Blow low, blow high,
Your haunting cry
For me, a wayfarer passing by;
Blow soft or keen,
I shall listen and lean
To catch what your whispered messages mean.

I shall hear, and heed
The voice of the reed,
And be glad of my kinfolk's word, indeed.
I shall hearken and hear
Your untroubled cheer
From the earth's deep heart, serene and clear.

Blow cold and shrill,
As the wind from the hill,
I yet shall follow to learn your will;
Blow soft and warm,
As an April storm,
I shall listen and feel my soul take form.

Blow glad and strong,
As the grosbeak's song,
And I mount with you over hurt and wrong;
Blow little and thin,
As the cricket's din;
But my door is wide, and I bid them in.

Blow, blow till there be
Inbreathed in me
Tinge of the loam and tang of the sea, —
A vagrom man,
Favoured of Pan,
Made out of ardour and sinew and tan,

With the seeing eye
For meadow and sky,
The want only beauty can satisfy,
And the wandering will,
The questing will,
The inquisitive, glad, unanxious will,

That must up and away

On the brave essay
Of the fair and far through the long sweet day, —
Of the fine and true,
The wondrous and new,
All the warm radiant bright world through.

Blow me the tune
Of the ripe red moon,
I shall sleep like a child by the roadside soon;
And the tune of the sun;
When our piping is done,
Lo, others shall finish what we have begun.

For the spell we cast
Shall prevail at last,
When fault is forgotten and failure past,
Prevail and restore
To earth once more
The lost enchantment, the wonder-lore.

And I must attain
To the road again,
With the wandering dust and the wandering rain, —
A sojourner too
My way pursue,
Who am spirit and substance, even as you.

Then give me the slow
Large will to grow,
As your fellows down by the brookside grow.
Ah, blow, and breed
In my manhood's need
The long sweet patience of flower and seed!

O pipes of Pan,
Make me a man,
As only your earthly music can;
And create in me
From your melody
The strength of the hills and the strength of the sea!

THE TIDINGS TO OLAF

This is a question arose in the Norseland long ago,
About the time of Yule, the season of joy and snow.
To-morrow, our Christmas Day, can you answer straight and true,

After these thousand years, when the question comes to you?

Olaf sat on his throne, and the priest of Thor stood by;
And the King's eyes were grey as the December sky.

"Whom shall we serve, O King the god of thy fathers, Thor,
Who made us lords of the sea, and gave us our land in war,

"Who follows our battle flag over the barren brine,
Who braces the bursting heart when the rowers bend in line,

"Who hath made us the fear of the world and the envy of the earth,
Whose splendour sustains us in death, who hath given us plenty for dearth,

"Or this poor, thought-ridden Jew, an outcast whose head was priced
At thirty pieces of silver, this friendless anarchist, Christ?

"Is not thine empire spread over the Western Isles?
Are not thy people sown wherever the sun-path smiles?

"Do there not come to thee iron and gems and corn?
Does not thy glory blaze wherever our trade is borne?

"Over the red sea-rim thy galleys go down with the sun;
Beyond the gates of the storm thy written mandates run.

"Behold, new lands arise to the lift of thy daring prows,
And health and riches and joy prosper thy fir-built house.

"Is there lack to thee of aught the strength of thy folk can give,
When the will and the longing come to stretch out thy hand and live?

"Honey and fruit and wine, are they not piled on the board?
Do not a hundred tribes pay tribute to our Lord?

Olaf, beloved of the gods! Is there an out-land tongue,
Is there an isle of the sea where thy praise has not been sung?

"Scarlet and silk and gold gleam on thy breast and brow.
Had the kings of the earth of old such honour and freedom as thou?

"Might and dominion and power and majesty, are they not thine?
Will the seed of warrior kings dishonour the war-god's shrine?

O King, do I speak this day in thy name, or forevermore
Let perish the ancient creed? By thy grace, is it Christ or Thor?"

Olaf sat on his throne. And the Priest of Thor gave place

To a pale dark monk. All eyes were bent on the stranger's face.

"O King, how shall I speak and answer this wisdom of eld?
Yet the new trees of the forest spring up where the old are felled.

"When the sombre and ancient firs are laid in the dust, in your North,
The tender young green of the birch and the delicate aspen put forth.

"Is the land left naked and bare, because the brush-fires have run?
Ye have seen the soft carpet of fern spread down where the blackening was done.

"With beauty God covers the ground, no acre too poor to befriend,
That thou and I and all men may perceive and comprehend.

"He carries the sea in His hand, He lights the stars in the sky,
And whispers over thy soul as the shadows move on the rye.

"The King has his kingly state, but his heart is the heart of man,
Swept over by clouds of grief, then sunlit with joy for a span.

"And every living spirit that is clothed with flesh and bone
Is just so much of God's being, His presence revealed and known.

"We are part of God's breath, as the gust, whereby thy hearth-fire is fanned,
Is part of the wild north- wind that rolls the breakers to land.

"We are a part of His life, as the waves are a part of the sea,
A moment uplift in the sun, then merged in eternity.

"What is it, O man and King, that stretches between us twain,
Like the living tides that gird the islands of the main?

"What lifts thy name, Olaf, aloft on the shout of thy folk in war?
What keeps it warm by the hearth? Is it the favour of Thor?

"No! 'Tis the love of thy people, the great common love of thy kind,
The thing that is old as the sun and stronger than the wind.

"And, Olaf, all these things, these goods which thy priest proclaims,
That make thee a lord among men, and give thee a name above names,

"Are gifts of the spirit of love. Take away love, and thy throne
Melts like a word on the air; thou art a name unknown.

"Is the King heavy at heart, and no man can tell him why;
What does his glory avail to put the heaviness by?

"But like any poor nameless man among men, the mighty King

Is heartened among his folk by the simple love they bring.

"Is the King weary in mind, and none can lighten his mood;
What cheers him to power anew but thought of his people's good?

"To love, to know, and to do! So we grow perfect apace,
The human made more divine, as the old to the new gives place.

"But who will show us the way, be lantern and staff and girth?
Where is the Light of the World and the Sweetness of the Earth?

"The King has a thousand men, yet one more brave than the rest;
The King has a hundred bards, yet one the wisest and best;

"The King has a score of friends, yet one most accounted of.
And now, if these three were one, in courage, in wisdom and love,

"There were the matchless friend, whose cause should enlist all lands,
Gentle, intrepid, and true. And there, O King, Christ stands.

"Freedom and knowledge and joy, not mine nor any man's,
But open to all the earth without proscription or bans,

"Where is the bringer of these? His hand is upon thy door.
And He who knocks, O King, is a greater God than Thor.

"Olaf, 'tis Yule in the world; the old creeds groan and fall,
The ice of doubt at their heart, the snows of fear over all.

"But now, even now, O friends, deep down in the kindly earth,
Are not the marvellous seeds awaiting the hour of birth?

"Even now in the sunlit places, do not the saplings prepare
To unfold their new growth to the light, unsheathe their rich buds on the air?

"And so, from the dark, sweet mould of the human heart will arise,
To enmorning the world with light and this life emparadise,

"The deathless, young glory of love. And valley and hill and plain
And fields and cities of men, they shall not sorrow again.

"For there shall be freedom and peace and beauty in that far spring,
And folk shall go forth without fear, and be glad at their work and sing.

And men will hallow this day with His name who died on the tree,
For the cause of eternal love, in the service of liberty.

"O King, shall the feet of Truth come in through thy open door,

Or alone out of all the world be debarred? Is it Christ or Thor?"

The King sat on his throne, and the two priests stood by.
And Olaf's eyes grew mild as a blue April sky.

Thus were the tidings to Olaf brought in the early days,
To be a lamp in his house, and a sign-post in the ways.

And you, O men and women, does it concern you at all,
That Truth still cries at the cross-roads, and you do not heed his call?

THE PRAYER IN THE ROSE GARDEN

Lord of this rose garden,
At the end of May,
Where thy guests are bidden
To tarry for a day,

Through the sweet white falling
Of the tender rain,
With thy roses theeward
Lift this dust again.

Make the heart within me
That crumbles to obey,
Perceive and know thy secret
Desire from day to day;

Even as thy roses,
Knowing where they stand
Before the wind, thy presence,
Tremble at thy hand.

Make me, Lord, for beauty,
Only this I pray,
Like my brother roses,
Growing day by day,

Body, mind and spirit,
As thy voice may urge
From the wondrous twilight
At the garden's verge,

Till I be as they be,
Fair, then blown away,
With a name like attar,

Remembered for a day.

www.ingramcontent.com/pod-product-compliance
Lightning Source LLC
Chambersburg PA
CBHW060100050426
42448CB00011B/2553